SIGHT WORD STORIES
& Seatwork Activities 2

REM 136B

A TEACHING RESOURCE FROM...

To find Remedia products in a store near you, visit:
http://www.rempub.com/stores

REMEDIA PUBLICATIONS, INC.
15887 N. 76TH STREET • SUITE 120 • SCOTTSDALE, AZ • 85260

TO THE TEACHER:

Sight Word Stories and Seatwork Activities is a collection of stories which utilize a list of nouns most commonly found in beginning readers. Each lesson is based on three or four nouns woven into a short story with seven related seatwork activities.

How To Use These Materials

Once the student is familiar with the procedure for completing each lesson, he or she can then complete subsequent lessons in the same manner.

Story:

The key nouns are highlighted in a box. The teacher may wish to introduce each word by pronouncing it for the students and elaborating by asking students to relate their own experiences with the word.

Questions:

Each story has several questions related to the content of the story just read.

Scanning:

Scanning is a reading skill which beginning readers can develop. They simply focus on a key word and count how many times that word appears in the story. (For purposes of consistency, students should count key words occurring in the title of the story, but not in the word box.)

Completion:

In this activity, students are given sentences with one word missing. The missing words are located in a list next to the sentences.

Choose the Word:

Students are presented with sentences that relate to the story. They must choose one of two words to complete the sentence properly, according to the story.

Sequencing:

This activity is a comprehension check of students' ability to remember the events in the story in correct sequence. Students indicate which event occurred first by numbering 1, 2, 3.

Yes/No:

This activity consists of sentences which do not necessarily relate to the story. The student indicates whether or not the sentence makes sense or could happen by writing "yes" or "no" in the blank following the sentence. For purposes of consistency in answering the questions, instruct the students to respond to the statements by writing "yes" if it could really happen, whether or not it happened in the story, and vice versa. For example, in many of the stories, animals are able to talk. However, if the student encountered a statement that said, "A cat can talk," they should answer it "no," because in real life cats do not talk.

Following Directions:

The final activity involves reading simple instructions and carrying out the directions. In most cases, this involves drawing an object, coloring it a specific color, and locating it in a certain place. The student is also given an opportunity to be creative by imagining what someone or something would say in the situation they just created.

Name _____

The Doll by the Door

There was a little boy doll that sat on a chair. The chair was by a door.

When someone would open the door, the door would make the little boy doll fall.

"OWW!" said the boy doll. "I do not like that door."

One day, a little girl came to the door. When she opened the door, the little boy doll fell down.

The girl said, "Little doll, sitting on a chair by the door is not good for you. You will fall. But I can help you."

The girl took the doll home and put the doll on her bed. "You will not fall now," said the girl.

The little boy doll said, "Good. I like to sit on the chair, but I will not fall here."

QUESTIONS:

1. What is the name of the story?

   _____

2. Where was the chair? _____

3. When someone would open the door, what did the doll do?

   _____

4. Did the doll like to fall? _____

5. Who came to help the doll? _____

6. Where is the doll now? _____

1

Name _____

SCANNING:

1. doll _____   3. chair _____

2. door _____   4. fall _____

COMPLETION:

1. A _____ doll sat on a chair.

2. The chair was _____ the door.

3. When someone would _____ the door,

   the doll would _____ .

4. A girl came to the _____ .

5. The girl said, "I can _____ you."

help
door
boy
open
fall
by

CHOOSE THE WORD:

1. A little _____ sat on a

   girl   **doll**

   _____ .

   chair   **door**

2. The chair was by the _____ .

   chair   **door**

3. The doll _____ like the door.

   did not   **did**

4. The girl took the doll to her _____ .

   home   **mother**

Name _____

SEQUENCING: (1 2 3)

_____ A doll sat by a door.

_____ The girl took the doll home.

_____ The doll fell off the chair.

YES/NO:

1. A doll can be little.   _____

2. A doll can sit on a chair.   _____

3. A chair can sit on a doll.   _____

4. A doll can be a boy doll.   _____

5. A girl can be a chair.   _____

6. A girl can be on a chair.   _____

7. A door can be by a chair.   _____

8. A doll can open a door.   _____

9. A door can be open.   _____

10. A house can have a door.   _____

11. A girl can sit by a door.   _____

12. A girl can open a door.   _____

FOLLOWING DIRECTIONS:

1. Draw a chair.
2. Draw a doll on the chair.
3. Color the doll's hair red.

4. Draw a dog by the chair.
5. Color the dog brown.
6. What is the doll saying?

3

dress
duck
ear
store

The Dress for a Duck

The girl did not feel well. She had something in her ear. It made her ear feel very bad.

The girl wanted to get a dress. She said to her mother, "May I get a dress?"

The mother said, "Yes. Get a dress with a duck."

The girl said, "A duck? Get a dress for a duck?"

The girl went to the store. She got a very little dress. She went home. She said to her mother, "Here is a dress for a duck. Will a duck want a dress?"

The mother said, "Oh, no. Not a dress FOR a duck; a dress with a duck ON it. We will take the dress back to the store. Then we will have someone take a look at your ear."

QUESTIONS:

1. How did the girl's ear feel? _____

2. What did the girl want to get? _____

3. What kind of dress did the girl's mother tell her to get?

_____

4. What did they do with the dress? _____

5. What is the name of the story?

_____

SCANNING:

1. dress _____   3. ear _____

2. duck _____   4. store _____

Name _____

COMPLETION:

1. I do not _____ very well today.

2. Do you like my new blue _____ ?

3. Let's go to the _____ .

4. The _____ is in the water.

5. There is something in my _____ .

6. The dress is very _____ .

dress
duck
store
ear
little
feel

CHOOSE THE WORD:

1. The girl did not _____ well.
   fell   **feel**

2. She had something in her _____ .
   ear   **eye**

3. The girl went to the store to get a _____ .
   duck   **dress**

4. The dress was very _____ .
   big   **little**

5. They will take the dress back to the _____ .
   store   **duck**

SEQUENCING: (1 2 3)

_____ They will take the dress back to the store.

_____ The girl got a very little dress.

_____ The girl had something in her ear.

5

STORY #2

YES/NO:

1. A duck can have a dress. _____

2. A mother can have a dress. _____

3. A girl can have an ear. _____

4. A duck can have an ear. _____

5. A girl can have a duck. _____

6. A girl can go to a store. _____

7. A duck can go to a store. _____

8. A girl can have a blue dress. _____

9. Something can be in a girl's ear. _____

10. A duck can be in a girl's ear. _____

11. A dress can be red. _____

12. A dress can be little. _____

13. A dress can have a duck on it. _____

14. A duck can have a dress on it. _____

15. A dress can have an ear. _____

FOLLOWING DIRECTIONS:

1. Draw a dress.
2. Color the dress yellow.
3. Draw a duck on the dress.
4. Draw a girl.
5. What is the girl saying?

elephant
eye
face
tail

The Elephant and His Tail

An elephant had a long, long tail. When he would walk, his tail would hit him in the face.

"This is not fun," said the elephant. "I do not like to get hit in the face."

One day, the elephant went for a walk. His tail hit him in the eye. Now he could not see.

The elephant sat down. "My eye hurts," he said. "My tail is just too long. What can I do?"

A little cat came up to the elephant. "I can help," she said. She did something to the tail of the elephant. "Now it will not hit you in the face," she said.

QUESTIONS:

1. What did his tail do when the elephant took a walk?

   _____

2. Did the elephant like to get hit in the face? _____

3. Who came up to help the elephant? _____

4. What is the name of the story?

   _____

SCANNING:

1. elephant _____   3. face _____

2. eye _____   4. tail _____

Name _____

COMPLETION:

1. The elephant has a very _____ tail.

2. The _____ is very big.

3. I have something in my _____ .

4. The dog has a very long _____ .

5. I got _____ with a ball.

6. The girl has a pretty _____ .

elephant
eye
face
tail
hit
long

CHOOSE THE WORD:

1. The elephant has a long, long _____ .
   face   **tail**

2. His tail would _____ him in the face.
   hug   **hit**

3. A little _____ came up to the elephant.
   cow   **cat**

4. She _____ the elephant.
   hit   **helped**

SEQUENCING: (1 2 3)

_____ An elephant had a very long tail.

_____ A little cat helped the elephant.

_____ The tail hit the elephant in the eye.

Name _____

YES/NO:

1. A tail has an eye. _____

2. A face has an eye. _____

3. A boy has an eye. _____

4. An elephant has an eye. _____

5. An elephant has a tail. _____

6. A boy has a tail. _____

7. A tail can be long. _____

8. A face can be long. _____

9. A dog has a tail. _____

10. A boy can hit a dog. _____

11. A boy can hit a boy. _____

12. An elephant can be big. _____

13. An elephant can be blue. _____

14. An elephant can ride on a boy. _____

15. A boy can ride on an elephant. _____

FOLLOWING DIRECTIONS:

1. Draw an elephant.
2. Draw a very long tail on the elephant.
3. Draw a happy face on the elephant.
4. What is the elephant saying?

9

feet
fire
fish
water

The Fish with Feet

A fish wanted to have feet. He wanted to get out of the water. He wanted to walk around.

"If I had feet, I could get out of the water," said the fish. "I could go all over. I could walk and run. I wish I had feet."

One day, the fish looked down. He had feet. "I have feet," said the fish. "I am so happy."

The fish walked out of the water. He walked on his feet. He walked by a big fire. The fire was very hot.

"I do not like fire," said the fish. "It is too hot."

The fish went away from the fire as fast as he could. "I am glad I have feet," said the fish. "My feet can take me away from the fire. I will go back to the water."

When the fish got back to the water, his feet were gone. "No more feet," said the fish. But the water was not hot like the fire. It was cold. The fish was happy.

QUESTIONS:

1. What did the fish want? _____

2. Did the fish like his feet? _____

3. Where did the fish walk? _____

4. Did the fish like the fire? _____

5. What is the name of the story?

_____

Name _____

SCANNING:

1. feet _____   3. fish _____

2. fire _____   4. water _____

COMPLETION:

1. A man can drink _____ .

2. A _____ is hot.

3. I have two _____ .

4. A _____ lives in water.

5. A man can _____ .

6. I _____ to swim in the water.

like
feet
fire
water
fish
walk

CHOOSE THE WORD:

1. A fish wanted to have _____ .
    fire   **feet**

2. He wanted to _____ around.
    walk   **ride**

3. The fish got _____ of the water.
    in   **out**

4. The fish walked by a _____ .
    feet   **fire**

5. The fish went back to the _____ .
    fire   **water**

SEQUENCING: (1 2 3)

_____ A fish wanted to have feet.

_____ A fish saw a fire.

_____ A fish walked out of the water.

YES/NO:

1. A man can live in water.   _____

2. A man can drink water.   _____

3. A man can drink fire.   _____

4. A fish can live in fire.   _____

5. Fire is hot.   _____

6. A man can eat a fish.   _____

7. A man can eat fire.   _____

8. A fire has feet.   _____

9. Water can be hot.   _____

10. A girl can have feet.   _____

11. A girl can live in water.

FOLLOWING DIRECTIONS:

1. Draw a lake.
2. Draw a fish in the water.
3. Draw a boy in the water.
4. What is the fish saying to the boy?

Name _____

The Flower in the Garden

A girl with long hair had a garden. She had one flower in her garden. It was a big, red flower.

"I like this flower," she said. "I like my garden. The flower makes the garden look so pretty."

The girl looked at the red flower. She looked at her long hair. Then she put the red flower into her hair.

"Now my hair will look pretty," she said. "What a pretty flower for my hair, but my garden is not pretty now. I wish I had a flower for my garden and a flower for my hair. Then I would have a pretty garden and pretty hair."

QUESTIONS:

1. What is the name of the story?

_____

2. What color was the flower in the girl's garden? _____

3. Did the girl like her garden? _____

4. Where did the girl put the flower? _____

5. Was the garden pretty after she picked the flower? _____

SCANNING:

1. flower _____   2. garden _____   3. hair _____

Name _____

COMPLETION:

1. A red flower is _____.

2. A flower grows in a _____.

3. The girl has long _____.

4. I gave my mother a pretty _____.

5. A _____ had a garden.

6. I _____ the flowers.

| flower |
| girl |
| garden |
| like |
| pretty |
| hair |

CHOOSE THE WORD:

1. A girl had long _____.
   feet   **hair**

2. She had a red_____ in her garden.
   fish   **flower**

3. The _____ was pretty.
   garden   **water**

4. The girl put the _____ into her hair.
   flower   **food**

5. The girl had _____ hair now.
   pretty   **garden**

SEQUENCING: (1 2 3)

_____ Now the garden is not pretty.

_____ The girl put the flower into her hair.

_____ The girl had a flower in her garden.

Name _____

YES/NO:

1. A flower can be red. _____

2. A girl can pick a flower. _____

3. A girl can eat a flower. _____

4. A girl can have long hair. _____

5. A flower can have long hair. _____

6. A girl can be in a garden. _____

7. A flower can be in a garden. _____

8. A flower can pick a girl. _____

9. A girl can eat a garden. _____

10. A girl can draw a flower. _____

11. A girl can draw a garden. _____

12. A girl can walk in a garden. _____

13. A fish can walk in a garden. _____

14. A flower can walk in a garden. _____

FOLLOWING DIRECTIONS:

1. Draw two flowers.
2. Color one flower yellow.
3. Color one flower purple.
4. Draw a girl.
5. Circle the flower that the girl will pick.

15

STORY #5

Name _____

The Black Hat

A man had a big, black hat. He put his hand into the hat and pulled out a little, white rabbit.

"Good-bye," said the rabbit, and the rabbit ran away.

The man put his hand back into the black hat. He pulled out a little, brown rabbit.

"Good-bye," said the brown rabbit, and it ran away, too.

The man said, "I do not like this. The white rabbit ran away. The brown rabbit ran away, too."

He put his hand into the hat again. This time, the man pulled out a little, gray squirrel.

"Are you going away?" said the man.

"No," said the gray squirrel. "There is a nut in your hat. I am staying right here."

QUESTIONS:

1. What did the man pull out of his hat first? _____

2. What did the man pull out of his hat next? _____

3. What did the rabbits say? _____

4. What color was the squirrel? _____

5. Did the squirrel go away, too? _____

6. What is the name of the story?

_____

Name _____

SCANNING:

1. hand _____   3. rabbit _____

2. hat _____   4. squirrel _____

COMPLETION:

1. A man had a _____hat.

2. The man had a _____on his head.

3. What is in your _____?

4. The _____ ate the nut.

5. The _____ hopped away.

6. A little _____ squirrel was in the hat.

hand
hat
black
rabbit
squirrel
gray

CHOOSE THE WORD:

1. A man had a _____ black hat.
         big   **little**

2. He put his _____ into the hat.
        head   **hand**

3. He pulled out a little, white _____.
        squirrel   **rabbit**

4. The rabbit _____ away.
      ran   **swam**

5. The squirrel had a _____ in the hat.
      rabbit   **nut**

                    STORY #6

Name _____

SEQUENCING: (1 2 3)

_____ The squirrel had a nut in the hat.

_____ The man pulled a rabbit out of the hat.

_____ The man had a big, black hat.

YES/NO:

1. A hat can be in a rabbit.   _____

2. A rabbit can be in a hat.   _____

3. A man can have a hat.   _____

4. A man can eat a hat.   _____

5. A hat can be black.   _____

6. A hat can eat a nut.   _____

7. A squirrel can eat a nut.   _____

8. A squirrel can be green.   _____

9. A man has a hand.   _____

10. A squirrel has a hand.   _____

FOLLOWING DIRECTIONS:

1. Draw a hat.
2. Color the hat red.
3. Draw something by the hat that can make you laugh.

Name _____

The Big Head

A man had a very big head. His head was so big that he did not like people to see him. He did not like his big head.

The man was very sad. One day, he got a letter. The letter said:

I have something for you.
It is for your head.
Come over right away.

Your friend

The man went to his friend. "I got your letter," the man said. "What do you have for my big head?"

The friend gave the man something. "Now you will not look like you have a big head."

What did the friend give the man?

QUESTIONS:

1. What is the name of the story?

   _____

2. Did the man like people to see him? _____

3. Why didn't the man like his head? _____

4. What did he get one day from a friend? _____

5. What did the friend give the man?   a ball?   a flower?   a hat?

   _____

Name _____

SCANNING:

1. man _____   3. letter _____

2. head _____   4. friend _____

COMPLETION:

1. A man got a _____ from his friend.

2. The boy and the _____ went for a walk.

3. You are a good _____ to me.

4. I put a hat on my _____ .

5. I feel very _____ today.

6. The friend had _____ for the man.

something
man
head
friend
letter
sad

CHOOSE THE WORD:

1. The _____ had a very big head.
      boy   **man**

2. He did not like his big _____ .
               head   **hand**

3. One day, he got a _____ from a friend.
            little   **letter**

4. The friend had something for the _____ .
                        man   **hat**

5. The friend gave the man a big _____ .
                        head   **hat**

Name _____

SEQUENCING: (1 2 3)

_____ A man did not like his big head.

_____ His friend gave him a big hat.

_____ The man got a letter from his friend.

YES/NO:

1. A hat has a head.   _____

2. A man has a head.   _____

3. A head can be big.   _____

4. A hat can be big.   _____

5. A man can be sad.   _____

6. A hat can be sad.   _____

7. A friend can get a letter.   _____

8. A hat can get a letter.   _____

9. A man can be a friend.   _____

10. A dog can be a friend.   _____

11. A man can have a big head.   _____

FOLLOWING DIRECTIONS:

1. Draw a boy.
2. Draw a friend.
3. Show something that the boy and the friend can do.

21   STORY #7

Name _____

The Horse on the Hill

A horse lived on top of a big hill. He was afraid to come down the hill. A big tree fell across the road. The horse did not want to jump over the tree.

Every day, a hen would bring the horse some hay. She would take the hay from the bottom of the hill to the top of the hill so the horse could eat.

One day, the hen said, "Horse, it is a long way down the hill to get the hay. It is a long, long way up the hill with the hay."

"I know," said the horse. "But I am afraid to jump over the tree to go down the hill."

"I jump over the tree every day to get you the hay," said the hen. "I jump over the tree to bring the hay up to you. I will not get your hay. If you want to eat hay, you will have to jump over the tree."

"The hay looks pretty good to me," said the horse. "I will learn to jump."

QUESTIONS:

1. Where did the horse live? _____

2. What did the hen bring to the horse? _____

3. What was the horse afraid to do? _____

4. What was the horse going to learn to do? _____

5. What is the name of the story?

_____

Name _____

SCANNING:

1. hay _____   4. horse _____

2. hen _____   5. tree _____

3. hill _____

COMPLETION:

1. The horse can eat a lot of _____ .

2. Let's walk up that big _____ .

3. The pretty, black _____ can run fast.

4. The boy was up in the _____ .

5. The _____ sat on the egg.

6. The horse can _____ over a tree.

| hill |
| jump |
| horse |
| hay |
| tree |
| hen |

CHOOSE THE WORD:

1. A horse lived on top of a big _____ .
   hill   **hen**

2. The horse did not want to _____ over the tree.
   run   **jump**

3. The hen would _____ hay to the horse.
   eat   **bring**

4. The hen wanted the horse to get the _____ .
   hay   **hat**

5. The horse will learn to _____ over the tree.
   tree   **jump**

STORY #8

Name _____

SEQUENCING: (1 2 3)

_____ The horse will learn to jump over the tree.

_____ The hen would bring the hay to the horse.

_____ The hen did not want to bring the hay to the horse.

YES/NO:

1. Hay can jump over a horse.   _____

2. A tree can jump over a horse.   _____

3. A hen can jump over a hill.   _____

4. A horse can go up a hill.   _____

5. A horse can go down a hill.   _____

6. A horse can eat hay.   _____

7. A man can eat hay.   _____

8. A hen can eat a horse.   _____

9. A man can go up a tree.   _____

10. A horse can go up a tree.   _____

11. A horse can walk down a road.   _____

12. A tree can walk down a road.   _____

FOLLOWING DIRECTIONS:

1. Draw a tree.
2. Color the tree green.
3. Draw a hen on top of the tree.

4. Draw a boy next to the tree.
5. What is the boy saying to the hen?

Name _____

The Kitten on the Farm

A girl and her father went to a farm. The girl saw a little black kitten on the farm.

"Look!" said the girl. "A little black kitten! May I take her home with me?"

"No," said the father. "We have a dog and a cat and a cow at home. We do not need a kitten. The kitten is happy here on the farm."

The kitten said to the father, "I do like the farm, but I like the girl, too. May I go home with you?"

The father said, "I did not know that a kitten could talk! You may go home with us — yes, yes, yes!"

QUESTIONS:

1. What is the name of the story?

    _____

2. Where did the girl and her father go? _____

3. What did the girl see on the farm? _____

4. Did the father want her to take the kitten? _____

5. Did the kitten want to go home with the girl? _____

6. Did the father let the kitten go home with them? _____

SCANNING:

1. farm _____   2. father _____   3. kitten _____

Name _____

COMPLETION:

1. A cow lives on a _____ .

2. A girl and her _____ went to the farm.

3. The girl saw a little black _____ .

4. The kitten could _____ .

5. The girl wanted to take the kitten _____ .

6. The father said they did not _____ a kitten.

home
need
farm
kitten
father
talk

CHOOSE THE WORD:

1. A girl and her _____ went to a farm.
    father   **mother**

2. The girl saw a little _____ kitten.
    brown   **black**

3. She wanted to take the kitten _____ with her.
    farm   **home**

4. The kitten wanted to go home with the _____ .
    girl   **boy**

5. The father did not know the kitten could _____ .
    talk   **walk**

SEQUENCING: (1 2 3)

_____ The father said the kitten could go home.

_____ The girl wanted to take the kitten home.

_____ A girl and her father went to a farm.

Name _____

1. A farm can go to a girl.   _____

2. A girl can go to a farm.   _____

3. A father can go to a farm.   _____

4. A girl can live on a farm.   _____

5. A kitten can live on a farm.   _____

6. A kitten can talk.   _____

7. A farm can talk.   _____

8. A girl can have a father.   _____

9. A farm can have a father.   _____

10. A kitten can have a father.   _____

11. A cow can live on a farm.   _____

12. A dog can live on a farm.   _____

13. A kitten can be black.   _____

14. A dog can be black.   _____

15. A cow can be black.   _____

FOLLOWING DIRECTIONS:

1. Draw a kitten.
2. Color the kitten black.
3. Draw a big dog by the kitten.
4. What is the dog saying to the kitten?

Name _____

| leg |
| milk |
| monkey |
| money |

Something for the Monkey

A monkey liked to drink milk. When boys and girls put money into his cup, he would dance on one leg. Then he would go and get some milk.

One day, a little boy came up to the monkey. "I would like to see you dance on one leg, monkey," he said, "but I do not have any money."

"That is o.k.," said the monkey. "You have something that you can put into my cup. It is not money, but I will dance on one leg for you."

The boy put milk from his cup into the monkey's cup. The monkey did his dance on one leg. "I do not want money," said the monkey. "I want milk!"

QUESTIONS:

1. What is the name of the story?

   _____

2. What did the monkey like to drink? _____

3. What did the boy want to see the monkey do?

   _____

4. Did the boy have any money? _____

5. What did the boy give the monkey? _____

SCANNING:

1. leg _____   3. monkey _____   5. monkey's _____

2. milk _____   4. money _____

Name _____

COMPLETION:

1. A monkey liked to drink _____ .

2. The monkey can _____ on one leg.

3. The boy hurt his _____ .

4. That is a funny _____ .

5. I have some _____ for you.

6. You must _____ all your milk.

leg
milk
money
monkey
dance
drink

CHOOSE THE WORD:

1. A monkey liked to _____ milk.
   eat   drink

2. He would dance on one _____ .
   leg   hand

3. A little _____ wanted to see the monkey dance.
   girl   boy

4. He did not have any _____ .
   monkey   money

5. The monkey liked the _____ the boy had.
   money   milk

SEQUENCING: (1 2 3)

_____ A boy wanted to see the monkey dance.

_____ The monkey wanted something that the boy had.

_____ The monkey danced for the boy.

STORY #10

Name _____

YES/NO:

1. Money can dance.   _____

2. A monkey can dance.   _____

3. Milk can dance.   _____

4. A boy can dance.   _____

5. A monkey can drink milk.   _____

6. A girl can drink milk.   _____

7. A girl can dance.   _____

8. Milk can have some money.   _____

9. A man can have some money.   _____

10. A man can have a monkey.   _____

11. A girl can see a monkey dance.   _____

12. A monkey can be a boy monkey.   _____

13. A girl can be funny.   _____

14. A monkey can be brown.   _____

15. Milk can be brown.   _____

FOLLOWING DIRECTIONS:

1. Draw a monkey.
2. Draw something a monkey likes to eat.
3. Color it yellow.

The Red Egg

In a little tree was a little, brown nest. In the nest was a big, red egg.

What was in the egg? For days and days, the egg just sat there. It did not open. It just sat there.

One day, it began to rain and rain and rain. The egg just sat there.

A girl and boy came by the tree. "Is my egg up there in the tree?" asked the boy.

"Yes," said the girl. "It is in the nest. I put it into the nest for you to find, but you did not find it.

The boy went up the tree and got the egg from the nest. "Let's get out of the rain," he said. "My red egg will get all wet."

"We will get wet, too," said the girl. "Let's run."

QUESTIONS:

1. Where was the egg? _____

2. What color was the egg? _____

3. Who put the egg into the nest? _____

4. Who got the egg from the nest? _____

5. What is the name of the story?

_____

SCANNING:

1. nest _____   2. egg _____   3. rain _____

COMPLETION:

1. The _____ is up in the tree.

2. The bird sat on the _____ in the nest.

3. The sun went away and now we have _____.

4. The boy climbed to the top of the _____.

5. The girl put the egg _____ the nest.

6. The _____wanted to get his red egg.

boy
nest
into
rain
egg
tree

CHOOSE THE WORD:

1. In a little tree was a _____ nest.
   green   brown

2. A big, red _____ was in the nest.
   bird   egg

3. A little _____ put the egg into the nest.
   girl   boy

4. The boy could not _____ the egg.
   find   eat

5. The boy went up the _____ and got the egg.
   rain   tree

SEQUENCING: (1 2 3)

_____ A girl and boy saw the egg in the nest.

_____ The girl and the boy ran to get out of the rain with the egg.

_____ The boy went up the tree to get the egg.

YES/NO:

1. An egg can rain. _____

2. A tree can rain. _____

3. A nest can be in the rain. _____

4. A nest can be in a tree. _____

5. An egg can be in a nest. _____

6. A girl can be in an egg. _____

7. A boy can eat an egg. _____

8. An egg can eat a boy. _____

9. A girl can run in the rain. _____

10. A nest can run in the rain. _____

11. A girl can sleep in a nest. _____

12. An egg can be big. _____

13. Rain can be fun. _____

14. A bird can have fun in the rain. _____

15. A nest can have fun in the rain. _____

FOLLOWING DIRECTIONS:

1. Draw a tree.
2. Draw a nest in the tree.
3. Draw two eggs in the nest.
4. Draw what is in the eggs.

STORY #11

Name _____

Pictures for a Party

A pig and a pony had a party. The pig had a picture for the pony, and the pony had a picture for the pig.

The pig said, "Here is a picture for you, pony." It was a picture of a big, red apple. "I thought you would like a picture of something good to eat."

The pony said, "And here is a picture you will like, my friend pig." It was a picture of some mud. "I thought you would like a picture of something good to play in!"

The pig said, "Good! Let's go outside and have this party in the back yard. There is a lot of mud for me and an apple or two for you."

"This is a great party," said the pony.

QUESTIONS:

1. What did the pig and the pony have? _____

2. What was the picture the pig gave the pony? _____

3. What was the picture the pony gave the pig? _____

4. Where did they go to have the party? _____

5. What is the name of the story?

_____

SCANNING:

1. party _____   3. pony _____   5. pictures _____

2. picture _____   4. pig _____

Name _____

COMPLETION:

1. The _____ is playing in the mud.

2. I like to ride the _____.

3. Here is a _____ of my dog.

4. Don't put your feet into the _____.

5. We will have a _____ for the girl.

6. This is a _____ party.

pig
pony
fun
mud
picture
party

CHOOSE THE WORD:

1. The pig and a _____ had a party.
   pony   **dog**

2. The pig had a picture of an _____ for the pony.
   egg   **apple**

3. The pony had a picture of _____ for the pig.
   rain   **mud**

4. The pig wanted to go _____ and play in the mud.
   in   **out**

5. The pony said that it was a _____ party.
   good   **bad**

SEQUENCING: (1 2 3)

_____ The pig and the pony wanted to go outside.

_____ The pony gave the pig a picture of some mud.

_____ The pig gave the pony a picture of an apple.

STORY #12

Name _____

YES/NO:

1. A pony can eat an apple.   _____

2. A pony can eat a pig.   _____

3. A boy can ride a pony.   _____

4. A pony can ride a pig.   _____

5. A pig can be fat.   _____

6. A pig can be big.   _____

7. A boy can draw a picture of a pig.   _____

8. A boy can draw a picture of a pony.   _____

9. A pony can ride on a girl.   _____

10. A boy can have a party.   _____

11. A girl can go to a party.   _____

12. A girl can eat an apple.   _____

13. An apple can be blue.   _____

14. An apple can draw a picture.   _____

15. An apple can be in a picture.   _____

FOLLOWING DIRECTIONS:

1. Draw a girl.
2. Draw an apple in one hand of the girl.
3. Draw a stick in the other hand of the girl.
4. Circle the hand that a pony will go to.

Name _____

The Rose and the Ring

A red rose and a yellow rose were in a garden. They liked to sit in the sun and talk.

One day, the yellow rose said, "I do not feel well today. The sun is making me hot. I am going to go to sleep."

The red rose said, "The sun should not make you go to sleep. The sun should make you happy. You must be sick."

A girl came into the garden. "Where is that yellow rose?" she asked. "My ring is in the rose."

The yellow rose was on the ground. It was very sick.

"Oh, no," said the girl. "Do not be sick, little flower. My ring is in you. That is why you do not feel well."

The girl picked up the yellow rose. In the rose was a little ring. "I did not mean to make you sick," she said. "You will be better now."

"I do feel better," said the yellow rose. "Put your ring on your finger, little girl."

QUESTIONS:

1. What is the name of the story?

   _____

2. Where were the red rose and the yellow rose? _____

3. How did the yellow rose feel? _____

4. Who came into the garden? _____

5. What had the girl put into the yellow rose? _____

Name _____

SCANNING:

1. rose _____   3. sun _____

2. ring _____   4. sick _____

COMPLETION:

1. The girl had a _____ on her finger.

2. I do not feel well today; I feel _____.

3. That is a pretty red _____.

4. I like the ring on your _____.

5. I like to be out in the _____.

6. I _____ hot in the sun.

sun
sick
rose
feel
ring
finger

CHOOSE THE WORD:

1. A red rose and a yellow rose were in a _____.
   green   garden

2. The yellow rose did not _____ well.
   feel   find

3. A _____ came into the garden.
   girl   boy

4. The girl had put a _____ into the flower.
   rose   ring

5. Now the _____ feels better.
   rose   sun

Name _____

SEQUENCING:

_____ The yellow rose feels better now.

_____ The yellow rose was sick.

_____ A girl had put a ring into the yellow rose.

YES/NO:

1. A rose can talk. _____

2. A rose can walk. _____

3. A rose can be in a garden. _____

4. A girl can pick a rose. _____

5. A rose can be yellow. _____

6. A rose can be red. _____

7. A girl can eat a rose. _____

8. A girl can have a ring. _____

9. A boy can have a ring. _____

10. The sun can be hot. _____

11. A rose can be in the sun. _____

12. The sun can eat a rose. _____

FOLLOWING DIRECTIONS:

1. Draw a rose.
2. Color the rose red.
3. Draw a pig.
4. Color the pig yellow.

5. Draw a ring.
6. Color the ring blue.
7. Circle the thing that you would give your mother for her birthday.

sheep
cold
shoe
snow

Shoes for the Sheep

A white sheep did not like the snow. "It is too cold," said the sheep. "I do not like to walk in the cold snow."

The farmer got mad at the sheep. "All of the other sheep go out in the snow," he said. "It is cold for them, too."

But the sheep did not want to go out. "It is just too cold," she said.

The farmer came up to the sheep. "Here is something for you," he said. "Put this shoe on this foot, and that shoe on that foot, and this shoe on that foot, and that shoe on this foot."

The sheep was happy. "I can walk in the snow now," she said. "My feet will be o.k. My ears are a little cold now!"

QUESTIONS:

1. What is the name of the story?

    _____

2. What didn't the sheep like to walk in? _____

    Why? _____

3. What did the farmer give the sheep? _____

4. Could the sheep walk in the snow now? _____

5. Now what was cold on the sheep? _____

Name _____

SCANNING:

1. sheep _____   3. snow _____

2. shoe _____   4. cold _____

5. shoes _____

COMPLETION:

1. That is a pretty, white _____.

2. It is too _____ to go outside.

3. The white _____ is very cold.

4. I have a big _____ on my foot.

5. I hurt my _____ playing outside.

6. The _____ has a lot of sheep.

| snow |
| shoe |
| sheep |
| cold |
| farmer |
| foot |

CHOOSE THE WORD:

1. A white _____ did not like the snow.
   farmer   **sheep**

2. The sheep said the snow was too _____.
   hot   **cold**

3. The farmer got _____ at the sheep.
   mad   **shoes**

4. The farmer got some shoes for the _____.
   foot   **sheep**

5. Then the sheep said that her _____ were cold.
   feet   **ears**

Name _____

SEQUENCING: (1 2 3)

_____ A sheep did not like the cold snow.

_____ The sheep said her feet were o.k. now.

_____ The farmer got some shoes for the sheep.

YES/NO:

1. A boy can have shoes.   _____

2. A sheep can have shoes.   _____

3. Shoes can be big.   _____

4. A cow can eat shoes.   _____

5. A sheep can walk in the snow.   _____

6. A farmer can walk in the snow.   _____

7. A farmer can have shoes.   _____

8. Feet can be big.   _____

9. Feet can be cold.   _____

10. Feet can be hot.   _____

FOLLOWING DIRECTIONS:

1. Draw something that can be cold.
2. Draw something that can be hot.
3. Draw something you like to do when it is cold outside.
4. Draw something you like to do when it is hot outside.

Name _____

The Toys

A little girl wanted to play with some toys. Her mother said, "You may have one toy. Pick a toy that you want."

The girl saw a little, black train on a table. Under the table, she saw a big, red wagon.

"I like the train," said the girl. "But I like the wagon, too."

"Just one," said her mother. "Not two toys."

The girl looked at the train on the table. She looked at the wagon under the table. "Just one?" she asked.

"Just one," said her mother.

Then a big girl came by. "I want the train on the table," she said. She took the train and went home.

"I will take the wagon under the table," said the little girl. "I will take it now before the big girl comes back and wants two toys."

QUESTIONS:

1. What is the name of the story?

   _____

2. How many toys could the little girl have? _____

3. What toy was on the table? _____

4. What toy was under the table? _____

5. What toy did the big girl take? _____

Name _____

SCANNING:

1. table _____   3. train _____

2. toys _____   4. wagon _____

                  5. toy _____

COMPLETION:

1. A _____ girl wanted to play with some toys.

2. I like to play with _____ , too.

3. The black _____ was on the table.

4. The red _____ was under the table.

5. We will eat at the _____ .

6. I can have only _____ toy.

> toys
> one
> table
> train
> little
> wagon

CHOOSE THE WORD:

1. A little girl wanted to _____ with some toys.
                           play   **see**

2. The girl saw a black _____ on a table.
                           train   **truck**

3. She looked at the _____ under the table.
                           wagon   **train**

4. A _____ girl came by and took the train.
           little   **big**

5. The little girl will take the _____ .
                           train   **wagon**

SEQUENCING: (1 2 3)

_____ The little girl will take the wagon.

_____ The big girl took the train.

_____ The little girl wanted to play with some toys.

YES/NO:

1. A table is a toy.   _____

2. A train can be a toy.   _____

3. A wagon can be red.   _____

4. A train can be red.   _____

5. A train can be big.   _____

6. A train can be little.   _____

7. You can eat a table.   _____

8. You can eat at a table.   _____

9. You can eat a train.   _____

10. You can eat on a train.   _____

FOLLOWING DIRECTIONS:

1. Draw a good toy for a girl.
2. Draw a good toy for a boy.
3. Draw something that is on a table.

Answer Key

PAGE 1: **Questions:** 1) The Doll by the Door 2) by the door 3) fall 4) no 5) a girl 6) on a bed

PAGE 2: **Scanning:** 1) 9 2) 8 3) 4 4) 4 **Completion:** 1) boy 2) by 3) open, fall 4) door 5) help
Choose the Word: 1) doll, chair 2) door 3) did not 4) home

PAGE 3: **Sequencing:** 1-3-2
Yes/No: 1) yes 2) yes 3) no 4) yes 5) no 6) yes 7) yes 8) no 9) yes 10) yes 11) yes 12) yes

PAGE 4: **Questions:** 1) bad 2) a dress 3) a dress with a duck 4) took it back to the store 5) The Dress for a Duck
Scanning: 1) 11 2) 8 3) 3 4) 2

PAGE 5: **Completion:** 1) feel 2) dress 3) store 4) duck 5) ear 6) little **Choose the Word:** 1) feel 2) ear 3) dress
4) little 5) store **Sequencing:** 3-2-1

PAGE 6: **Yes/No:** 1) no 2) yes 3) yes 4) yes 5) yes 6) yes 7) no 8) yes 9) yes 10) no 11) yes 12) yes 13) yes 14) no 15) no

PAGE 7: **Questions:** 1) hit him in the face 2) no 3) cat 4) The Elephant and His Tail
Scanning: 1) 7 2) 3 3) 3 4) 6

PAGE 8: **Completion:** 1) long 2) elephant 3) eye 4) tail 5) hit 6) face
Choose the Word: 1) tail 2) hit 3) cat 4) helped **Sequencing:** 1-3-2

PAGE 9: **Yes/No:** 1) no 2) yes 3) yes 4) yes 5) yes 6) no 7) yes 8) yes 9) yes 10) yes 11) yes 12) yes 13) no 14) no
15) yes

PAGE 10: **Questions:** 1) feet 2) yes 3) by a fire 4) no 5) The Fish with Feet

PAGE 11: **Scanning:** 1) 11 2) 6 3) 12 4) 6 **Completion:** 1) water 2) fire 3) feet 4) fish 5) walk 6) like
Choose the Word: 1) feet 2) walk 3) out 4) fire 5) water

PAGE 12: **Sequencing:** 1-3-2 **Yes/No:** 1) no 2) yes 3) no 4) no 5) yes 6) yes 7) no 8) no 9) yes 10) yes 11) no

PAGE 13: **Questions:** 1) The Flower in the Garden 2) red 3) yes 4) into her hair 5) no **Scanning:** 1) 10 2) 8 3) 7

PAGE 14: **Completion:** 1) pretty 2) garden 3) hair 4) flower 5) girl 6) like
Choose the Word: 1) hair 2) flower 3) garden 4) flower 5) pretty **Sequencing:** 3-2-1

PAGE 15: **Yes/No:** 1) yes 2) yes 3) no 4) yes 5) no 6) yes 7) yes 8) no 9) no 10) yes 11) yes 12) yes 13) no 14) no

PAGE 16: **Questions:** 1) white rabbit 2) brown rabbit 3) Good-bye 4) gray 5) no 6) The Black Hat

PAGE 17: **Scanning:** 1) 3 2) 6 3) 7 4) 2 **Completion:** 1) black 2) hat 3) hand 4) squirrel 5) rabbit 6) gray
Choose the Word: 1) big 2) hand 3) rabbit 4) ran 5) nut

PAGE 18: **Sequencing:** 3-2-1 **Yes/No:** 1) no 2) yes 3) yes 4) no 5) yes 6) no 7) yes 8) no 9) yes 10) no

PAGE 19: **Questions:** 1) The Big Head 2) no 3) too big 4) letter 5) a hat

PAGE 20: **Scanning:** 1) 6 2) 7 3) 3 4) 4 **Completion:** 1) letter 2) man 3) friend 4) head 5) sad 6) something
Choose the Word: 1) man 2) head 3) letter 4) man 5) hat

PAGE 21: **Sequencing:** 1-3-2 **Yes/No:** 1) no 2) yes 3) yes 4) yes 5) yes 6) no 7) yes 8) no 9) yes 10) yes 11) yes

PAGE 22: **Questions:** 1) top of a big hill 2) hay 3) to jump over the tree 4) jump 5) The Horse on the Hill

PAGE 23: **Scanning:** 1) 9 2) 3 3) 8 4) 8 5) 6 **Completion:** 1) hay 2) hill 3) horse 4) tree 5) hen 6) jump
Choose the Word: 1) hill 2) jump 3) bring 4) hay 5) jump

PAGE 24: **Sequencing:** 3-1-2 **Yes/No:** 1) no 2) no 3) no 4) yes 5) yes 6) yes 7) no 8) no 9) yes 10) no 11) yes 12) no